FINISHING LINE PRESS

www.finishinglinepress.com

Preserve

poems by

Susan Kolodny

Finishing Line Press
Georgetown, Kentucky

Preserve

ACKNOWLEDGMENTS
With grateful acknowledgments to the editors of the following journals in which
versions of these poems first appeared:

Edgz: "Croc"
Marlboro Review: "Little Frog" and "*Lory Lorius Garrulus*"
The English Journal: "Hippos" and "Troop"
Stoneboat: "Counterintuitive"

My love and thanks to Brooks Haxton, Elizabeth Robinson, Robert Thomas,
and Susanne Dyckman for their friendship, generosity, and help—editorial and
otherwise—with this book. In memory of Steve Kowit who, upon reading a few
of these poems, argued passionately for the dignity of hippos. He is greatly missed.
To Helen Fremont for her encouraging and thoughtful comments on an early
draft. To Elaine Miller Bond, fellow animal lover and writer, for her help with
cover design. To dear Noah, Sarah, Gemma, bright little light, and Luca for all
sorts of reasons. In memory of my mother, Helen, who, at a tidepool when I was
seven asked me to describe what I saw and so taught me that describing fosters
seeing; I see that tidepool still. And, always, to Lewis, cherished companion over
all our miles and years.

Publisher: Leah Maines

Editor: Christen Kincaid

Cover Art: Lewis Finneburgh

Author Photo: Lewis Finneburgh

Cover Design: Elizabeth Maines McCleavy and Elaine Miller Bond

Printed in the USA on acid-free paper.
Order online: www.finishinglinepress.com
        also available on amazon.com

Author inquiries and mail orders:
Finishing Line Press
P. O. Box 1626
Georgetown, Kentucky 40324
U. S. A.

Table of Contents

I.

II.

III.

For Lewis—my companion on the journey—and the guides

In wildness is the preservation of the world.

Henry David Thoreau

I.

Arrival

Xakanaxa Camp, Moremi Preserve

The guide, meeting our tiny plane
on the landing strip, says
"You must show your passports
to the airport police." Where,
we ask—savannah is all we see—
are the airport police?
He grins. We follow his gaze
to the wildebeest who
"considers this strip his."
What border are we crossing?

Little Frog

Little frog, we'd have missed you,
but for the boatman
who reached out with his pole, touched
the wheat-white bulrush stalk,
and there you were, thumb-sized,
a translucent gray-brown-green,
breathing its sweet scents
and clinging to the slender,
swaying world.

Botswana : An Introduction

I am first in line for breakfast

                on the safari camp deck.

The woman serving

                fills a bowl

with cereal and fruit

                and places it on the railing

behind her before she turns to me.

                I am puzzled,

a bit put off   until two

                turquoise-breasted birds

alight on the railing, then the bowl,

                and begin to eat.

Startled Grace

You are the first animals we see,
such delicate limbs and markings—
thin black stripes on fine faces,
small rumps, hind legs. Here,
then there, in herds of eight or nine.
Soon no one calls out "Impala"
yet we stop when you appear
to see again your startled grace,
how you dart and arc away
or stand motionless and gaze out at us
as we come upon you, gaze
warily. May we—the fifteenth,
the fiftieth time—always newly see you.

A Tower of Giraffes

Faces in the top
still-leafy branches
sweet, long lashes,
mouths puckering.
Tufted knobs
atop their heads,
jutting ears,
elongated necks, bony
legs, vanish into trees.
The tallest
is missing his tail—
a lion probably.
All browse
unconcerned
in the long dry season,
lions also hungry,
near.

Croc

How thoughtful of you
to stretch out in the sun just
under the Beware
of the Crocodile sign.
You watch us, waiting, near,
toothy, narrow headed,
with one open eye.

Hippos

How can anything with such
a comical voice, like
silly laughter rising from the river—
chuff, chuff, chuff, woo woo—
such silly ears, such love
of mud and muck, be
the most dangerous
four-legged animal
in Africa, cause
of the greatest number
of human deaths?
This gray, truck-sized lump
that stands yawning
shoulder-deep in water half
its life, eats grass, *woo woos,*
and flicks its little ears?
Ah, should you,
when he's out grazing,
cross his escape route
to the river, he'll run you over
or bite you in half.

Okavango Meditation

The sun hangs red
behind an acacia.
Reedbucks—horns
short, swept back—
and an ostrich
graze the savannah.
Mind, slowed, discovers
its intricate course
not as herds do. As,
at the start of the rainy season,
the waters flowing south
from Angola discover,
spill into, re-shape
the Okavango's six thousand-
square mile splendor,
its lagoons, lakes,
channels, its rivers.

Herd, or A Dazzle of

All those Berkeley teens
with their piercings, tattoos,
studded dog collars,
spiked hair tinted green
won't be much to look at
after these striped—even their faces
and paintbrush manes—
four-legged locals grazing
in the African grass,
each distinctive without trying
(they call them "a dazzle"),
each a work in black and white.

Monso

After he has shown us the sleeping pride,
baboons spilling from the trees,
a lone bull elephant, gray-crowned cranes
and sacred ibis along the river,
the duplex nest of marabou stork
built out over the lagoon,
eland, waterbucks, kudu,
all protected by law
and in their native, pristine habitat,
I ask him where he grew up.
He tells me *here*, in Moremi,
before it became a preserve and his people
were made to move into town.
We sit quietly for a moment in the truck.
Then, like a lord come back
to work on his estate
because its confiscation left him broke
and homeless, graciously
he shares his pleasure in the hidden places
he has known since boyhood.

Paradise

Off road, we stop.
An elephant strolls past.
A lavender-breasted bird—a roller—
lights on a nearby bush.
Five zebras and a wildebeest
graze in the grasses opposite.
This section of the park
is known as Paradise.
On a branch above,
five hooded vultures.

Sixty

We sit single file
in the *mokoro*.*
The boatman
stands behind us
with his pole.
Between banks,
water lilies,
each an offering
on a single stem.
Then, constellations
of water lilies.

Today   I   am   sixty.

Grasses and the water's
dark surface, its
ripples, conceal
roots, predators.
The channel narrows.
In the marsh
beyond, a bull elephant
knee-deep in water,
cools himself
with a slow back
and forth of his ears.

*A canoe of the Okavango Delta.

Traveling Companions

For three days, we've shared the guide
and truck, watched lions hunt, elephants
at their bath. They're honeymooners,
slightly older than our children,
well-traveled, schooled, bright.
We sense what a passionate time they're having,
and like them for it even more.
We can be silent together, or talk.
I know they like my husband's bluntness
and his humor. Still, I see her wonder,
this quick, competent young woman,
perhaps at how I forget the names of things,
though she enjoys the poems I quote.
Our last day, she asks, "Do you work?"
"Yes," I say *(may this not change our ease
or conversation)*, "I'm a psychoanalyst."
She smiles. "Now *that*
puts things in quite a different light."
I think I know what she means.
Meaning gives way to moment,
and we go on like old friends, delighting
in red lechwe, some warthogs,
an intently-staring-back-at-us giraffe.

Lory Lorius Garrulus

Green wings do not match
    your red body.
You are an often-repaired
    car with unmatched
        paint on its front doors.
Beautiful unmatched
    paint. Beautiful doors.

Ancient Enemy

Stretched out asleep
in the sand
and grass
with your splotched
olive, buff,
and brown print,
each scale
relaxed. We
almost didn't
see you
in the shade,
did, froze
in the truck
to watch
you nap.
For a moment
almost as curious
about you,
p y t h o n,
as afraid.

Sunset, Moremi

Remember, we're in their territory, not ours.
Xakanaxa Safari Camp Director

From intently watching hippos
in the river, we glance up:
sky a pink fire, sun
a molten red flat sinking disk.
The elephant-ravaged trees—
paper silhouettes
absorbing the ink of nightfall.
Vultures perched above
stiffen into gargoyles.
The sun's final red
bleeds into the water.
A nearby roar, a barking
return us to the steel-framed
confines of the truck.

Breaking Bread

I had not wanted to sit with them.
Their language, which we heard
as we entered,
is guttural, and for me
forever full of shudders.
But by the time
we'd had dinner and talked,
they of the leopard,
we of the lions and the python that day,
and of our "leaders,"
I had unclenched my jaw
and had even
begun to laugh with them.
The safari camp director
announced my sixtieth birthday
with a cake, and they
sang Happy Birthday
in that language not just of Hitler,
but of Rilke.
Outside, thunder:
a possible early ending
to the dry season.

II.

Selinda Camp

Four days crossing desert
and bush. Now, a morning
in shade outside our tent.

A tsessebe passes
on a solitary errand.

A gray bird with a scimitar beak
on the tent porch railing.

A pair of warthogs trot by
in single file late for a meeting.

And the two of us
in the October heat

content to be mere specks
under African skies,

and awed
as at our species' dawning.

Restraint

An elephant sauntering past
our stopped truck
pauses to rub one skinny flank
against a tree. She unfurls
her ears. Her trunk is curled.
In it—provoked, she could smash us
and the truck—she carries
a branch bouquet of green.

Vultures

They perch
in shabby uniforms
to wait
for what comes next.
We shudder
and drive on.

Cape Buffalo

With your small brain and
massive body, your sharp
horns, you are a heavily armed
country led by a fanatic who
feels menaced by a shadow
and will attack first.

Crafts Market

I escape the local merchants
trying desperately to sell me identical
soapstone hippos each insists
he has carved himself, as taught
by a now-blind uncle in his village.
I sit on a cement ledge far enough away
to be left undisturbed and pour water
over my head. October is so hot
they call it "suicide month."
A gray vervet monkey squats nearby.
He watches, too. He is not a tourist,
entranced with the "exotic," able
to leave it on the next flight out. He
need not chide himself for being curious,
for viewing the marketplace urgency as theater.

Rhino Beetle

What brings you to my face towel,
shiny beetle? On this hot
African night? And where
have you lost your horn?
Your carapace gleams,
a polished grooved stone.
Its halves unhinge,
split into wings, and you
who once crawled now fly.

Guest

Something is near
I flip on the flashlight
I am staring at
and stared at   startled by
and have startled   what?
A ferret face   whitish
cat fur   dark
spots   a ringed tail.
Knocking our toothpaste   off
                              the sink
it scurries up the canvas wall
into the night   this
(we learn)   baby
genet   drawn by our voices
by the curiosity that is
a kind of love.
It drew us   too
to meet these others
and   to learn their names.

Troop

I ask our guide the collective noun
for these baboons we watch descend
like a sudden shower from the trees,
gather, and line up. "A troop."
Ah, but in this troop—as the females
scoop up and hold their young, the young
not already clinging to their mother's belly—
when the alpha appears, huge, imposing,
wearing his status like a uniform with medals,
he does not command the rest to kill, or die.
He does not charge, or send them into battle.
He picks up the one infant unattended,
and with a chiding look, hands it to its mother,
steps forward and stands facing us alone,
his back to all the rest, massive shoulders raised,
chest out, chin lowered, as they march behind him,
into the denser woods beyond. Only when his troop
has dissolved into the farther trees
does this commander-in-chief,
with nothing more to do just now or prove,
turn, and with regal indifference to us strut away.

Saddle-Billed Stork

Bill bright yellow,
red-orange, and black,
colors of the beads
someone brought me once
from Kenya. You take
a few stork steps
along the Namibian shore,
stop, unfurl your wings
and stand—*Il Maestro*, baton
poised to start the orchestra,
balancing on long
red-jointed stilts.

Bank

Currency here   is *pula*   word
for rain   I have come
to this bank   to partake
of its wealth—   its
black-winged stilt   Egyptian
geese   yellow-billed stork   its
crocodiles   impersonating logs
its silver and   copper grasses
its river   in the October light
a gleam of obsidian   flecked   gold.

Through Binoculars

Chobe National Park

One comes   tusks first
into   the open
space   her trunk
curled towards
her mouth   then
a row of trunks
and tusks
a pair   of ears
swung wide
as saloon doors.
All veer
in single file
past the sausage tree.
From afar   a caravan
of swaying trunks
and ropy tails
between towering
wrinkled sides.

Breakfast Meditation

The fierce-eyed African fish
eagle perched
over the Chobe River
watches two
shirtless fishermen with nets
and canoe push off
from the conical village
on the Namibian shore
and row—muscles
and the water's ripples
in rhythm—turns its head
to watch a tourist barge
on the Botswana side
drift nearer
the submerged bloat
of hippos just upriver.
Gazes   scans
until prey spotted   hunger
pressing it yelps piercingly and soars.

"Adrenaline Grass"

Three days after the kill
the pride begins to stir
from its long postprandial
sleep. The old lion turns slowly
towards us. His great jaw
with its huge
incisors opens, shuts.
He rises and lumbers
toward the river.
Three lionesses lift their heads
over the waking cubs
to sniff the air
as we might read a menu.
They stand, ears alert,
sinews growing taut, slink
into the lion colored, lion-high
Adrenaline Grass.
A wildebeest stops grazing
and looks up. The savannah,
impartial, waits.

He Who Does Not Remember History

Despite their tusks,
low, stout bodies,
funny, upright tails,
the two young warthogs
huddled together look
desolate. The mothers
abandon them early,
go off again to mate
and produce more young,
only to abandon those
in turn. The two
lean towards each other,
left on the savannah
as they will later leave
their own, unguarded
among predators, amid
scattered bones and dung.

Hyena

Muzzle dark, head
low, its gaze on us.
We had not thought
an animal, except
humans, could loathe.

Muse

Outside André's window
a large moth
orbits the porch light.
What its flutter
has brought
springs onto the sill inches
from where André sits,
lowers herself
onto her haunches,
eyes fixed on the moth,
fur sleek, gorgeous with its rosettes
of spots, long tail curled
against the glass.
She bats at the moth
with each pass. André longs
to call out to his wife.
An audible breath
could bring the leopard
through the half open window
onto his desk,
or make her vanish
in the night.

Bones

We ask B.B. to stop
beside the scattered bones.
He stops. He has shown us sunsets
splendid as anywhere on earth.
Elephants with their new calves bathing.
The pride of fourteen lions
blood-sated and asleep.
Now these bones the lions,
then the dogs have feasted on,
and the vultures and the insects
in their turn picked clean.

We study them. What we dread,
hyenas eat and digest,
excreting a white powder
with their droppings, recycling
calcium from bones.

III.

Kazungula Crossing
Zambia

All shimmer like mirages:
massive-cabbed flatbed trucks
hauling logs, tanks of gasoline.
Men in suits
despite the awful heat.
Three boys, bare legs dusty,
with a set of djembe drums.
A man in purple tee and pink
shorts pushing a cart
of green bananas.

A   still   space.

A woman in a bright orange
and navy
block-print dress
and head-wrap, rugs piled
on her head. She is tall,
erect. She passes us
on this land
she knows is hers
as a stream
over pebbles, grass.

Ellie Park*

We stand with "Africa"
on the banks of the Zambezi.
He calls out, "Bob, Betty, Danny,
Miralou, Elaine." One by one
they appear from the stand of trees
on the island opposite,
enter the river, swim across,
silently ascend.
Silently they walk—
how can animals so large
make no sound?—towards us.
Bob, the first, the lead male, slows,
stops where I stand, dwarfed.
His tusks, trunk rest inches
from my now-pounding heart.
Africa tells them,
again naming each,
"go to the corral." These
massive animals, like planets, turn
but make no sound.
Nor do I, in awe.

*A preserve where orphaned elephants are cared for and
human visitors given an opportunity to interact with them.

Monitor Lizard: A Timeline of Life on Earth

He comes—five feet long,
in mold-gray chainmail
and on spiky lizard toes, claws
clicking—up the single step
to our safari tent porch
where we stand, just arrived,
and shudder at his sudden
scaly appearance up
and across in front of us,
shudder at his equally abrupt
disappearance (though not
from visceral memory),
like past eras and lost species,
back down into tall grass.

Ostrich

Assembled of used spare parts
by a maker slightly distracted
or merely playing around,
your movements—that jerky
strut on skinny plucked legs—
your too-ornate hind plumage.
No wonder you hide
your head in the sand.
Or sprint   jet-fast   from   us.

Carapace

A large oval rock—
brown, yellow, and black
concentric, raised patterns
on its surface—lies
by the river in the grass.

From it venture
a square
protruding head,
claw-like tail,
four pebbly feet.

It turns its head side
to side and evidently
not pleased,
retracts all
and resumes being

a large,
oval
intricately-
patterned
rock.

Display

A male calf, almost mature,
seeing we are yards away
in our boat and pose no threat,
extends his ears, raises his trunk,
kicks in the dirt, trumpets.
His mother—she
would charge in earnest
if we came near—watches,
concealed but for one great ear
in the nearby stand of trees.

[To] Ruminate

From dense grass
halfway to the sky, her spindly
legs, chestnut and tan
mosaic coat, tower neck,
sweet ears, knobbed head,
face lifted towards
the uppermost branch
in contemplation of the light.

Counterintuitive

Who or what
invented you?
You wear none
of the camouflage
of your fellow creatures.
Giraffe vanishes
into trees, reedbuck
into gold grass. You
are a psychedelic poster—
compact muscular body,
seemingly painted
pinwheel stripes.
Amidst all this gold, buff
and olive,
they are audacious black
and white. Your
main predator
sees in black and white
and gets confused
when you move.
Unlike most, you do well
to go where you will,
standing boldly out.

Spring Hare

In the flashlight beam
we see his long, nacreous
inner ears, miniature
forelegs like a kangaroo's,
then the hind-leg-powered
leap. I'd thought his name
referred to the season, not
to the single bound
that catapults him
to whatever may await
within the next
concealing patch of green.

Victoria Falls in the Dry Season

It is like trying to imagine
the elderly in their youth.

Less a roar now
than an
echo, the vast
falls that
they tell us
in June
were a
mile-wide
rush and wall
of water, mist
and thunder,
diminished
in the dry season—
scattered slim
white veils,
sparse threads
over the
largely bare
and scarred
descending walls
of rock.

The Leap
Victoria Falls

He is about fifty, balding,
and doesn't look
especially courageous.
But today, as friends
rode elephants past
cape buffalo, he
went to the platform
over the Falls
where you sign up,
and decided to do it—
to step out over
the abyss, held by a cord.

He sits smiling
as drinks are served
on this porch above the Zambezi.
And we, strangers touched
by his quiet pleasure
in something overcome,
raise our glasses to him.
And to this continent's
bloody, dazzling beauty—
the *source*—
its promise of redemption
to all of us who come.

"Suicide Month"

In the October heat
of "Suicide Month,"
frogs and hippos
chatter in the river.
A thousand beetles
thrum against our screen.
They beat and hiss
into the lamp.
Something growls,
something answers.
From our tent
we join the chorus.
We're here, too, alive.

River Club

Zambia

A man pushes a wheelbarrow

down the path by the river,
past flower beds,
the guest chateaux.

He pauses in a break
between garden sheds.
He seems to think he is unseen.

The wheelbarrow is empty.
He leans on it as if it held
all his air and light.

"Johnson,"

says his name tag, this young man
who brings our drinks
onto the colonial veranda.
Though shy, when we smile
he smiles warmly back.
When he sees we don't wish only
to be waited on, he asks
where we're from and what
kinds of animals we have
in our country. Startled,
I say bears, horses,
a different kind of buffalo
from theirs. He asks
have we seen whales and
what do they look like.
I try ineptly to draw him one.
How big are they, he asks? We say,
pointing to the banquet table,
ten times as long as that.
He shakes his head. We talk of oceans,
which he hopes one day to see.
He has a friend in America who
writes to him of snow and mountains.
We talk of the coming U.S.
elections. He is well informed
and has clear views about them,
he listens to the BBC, and reads.
The African sun glides
behind the horizon. Johnson
needs to help get dinner. He says
he hopes to see us at breakfast,
clears our glasses, sweetly asks
if he might keep "the sketch."

Host

The grounds are lush, the staff
gracious and proficient. In the lounge,
a well-varnished grand piano,
a leather-bound set of Dickens.
Some framed colonial era photographs.
Roger, who manages these "chateaux"
on the Zambezi, orders his staff
to move the dining table outside
where it is cooler, onto the grass.
He sits at the head, this
Oxford-educated *raconteur*.
By dessert, he is telling a history
of Livingston. My skin prickles.
He speaks of the Jews, "those rich
merchants with their famous skill
at making money." Then, despite
his nearby, courteous Zambian staff,
of the "Africans, their
lack of discipline or will to work."
I crumble my biscotti
into crumbs, then particles.
Nearby, jacaranda blossoms glow
with moonlight. Hyenas devour bones.

Youth and Age

The young Brits, staying
as we are at the chateaux
along the Zambezi,
emerge from the Livingston
craft shop hauling a metal-strip
sculpture of a warthog, about
two-and-a-half feet long
and half-a-foot wide.
I looked at them, too,
but I am too old and practical
to be hauling a metal warthog half
around the world. Unfazed
as we tease them about how
they'll get it home,
they decide their warthog
will be lonely in the London flat
and go back in to get it
a mate. Later we see them
at the Jo'burg Airport,
hauling their unwieldy
souvenirs and laughing,
as they will be—and we envy
that they will—all the long way
back to London, and home.

Departure Gate

She paces in weary arcs
between airline service windows,
making increasingly
urgent calls on her phone.
Even her clothes
appear to be unraveling.
She is not my sister.
Or my neighbor. Can't
someone *else* observe
and attend to her
before her fragile hold
gives way?
We may not speak
the same language.
I don't even know
whom to call
to say pardon me,
there is a woman
about to fall apart
in your airport. Send
some help.
I am a foreigner here.
A tourist. *Surely*
this—other—isn't my concern.

Leaving Africa

Tomorrow we will be back
under a roof, among
humans, many of them tedious
creatures who, unlike
these denizens
of savannah and bush
that the guides
help us to see and help
preserve, can go around
for years not noticing
a thing. Not even
that they are lonely and afraid.
That the day grows dark.
The ascent steep. The predators
circle us. The levees
are down. The river, rising.

Preserve
For Henry

Soon, I think, they'll vanish—
the pride of lions sleeping in the grass,
the wildebeest on the landing strip,
storks and sacred ibis along the rivers.
But no. I close my eyes and they
are there. I will not lose Africa.
It will become, for me,
like those we've lost who,
once mourned, live on inside us.
Presences, they comfort and caution.
Guides, they help us to see
and love the astonishing—the small,
the vast, what is in view, what hidden—
all that we meet along the way.

Susan Kolodny's poems appear in *New England Review, Beloit Poetry Journal, Bellingham Review*, and in other journals and several anthologies. Her work has been featured on Poetry Daily and American Life in Poetry. Her first collection, *After the Firestorm*, was published in 2011 by Mayapple Press. She has an MFA in poetry from the Program for Writers at Warren Wilson College, a Doctorate in Mental Health from UC Berkeley-UCSF, and she is a graduate of the San Francisco Psychoanalytic Institute. The author of *The Captive Muse: On Creativity and Its Inhibition* (PsychoSocial Press, 2000), Kolodny has lectured and taught widely on creativity and what gets in its way. She is a Member and Faculty at the San Francisco Center for Psychoanalysis where she developed and chairs an event series called "Poetry and Psychoanalysis." When not traveling to see what she can of the world and its creatures or spending time with family, she writes and practices in Oakland. *Preserve* is her second collection.